MW00573925

PANDEMIC AFTEREFFECTS

THE SURGE IN TEEN EATING DISORDERS

KATIE SHARP

ReferencePoint Press®

San Diego, CA

© 2023 ReferencePoint Press, Inc.
Printed in the United States

For more information, contact:
ReferencePoint Press, Inc.
PO Box 27779
San Diego, CA 92198
www.ReferencePointPress.com

LIBRARY OF CONGRESS CATALOGING-IN-PUBLICATION DATA

Names: Sharp, Katie John, author.
Title: Pandemic aftereffects : the surge in teen eating disorders / by
   Katie Sharp.
Description: San Diego, CA : ReferencePoint Press, 2023. | Includes
   bibliographical references and index.
Identifiers: LCCN 2021061317 (print) | LCCN 2021061318 (ebook) | ISBN
   9781678203443 (library binding) | ISBN 9781678203450 (ebook)
Subjects: LCSH: Eating disorders in adolescence--Psychological
   aspects--Juvenile literature. | Eating disorders in
   adolescence--Treatment--Juvenile literature. | Epidemics--Psychological
   aspects.
Classification: LCC RJ506.E18 S52 2023 (print) | LCC RJ506.E18 (ebook) |
   DDC 616.85/2600835--dc23/eng/20211221
LC record available at https://lccn.loc.gov/2021061317
LC ebook record available at https://lccn.loc.gov/2021061318

CONTENTS

AS A PANDEMIC RAGES, EATING DISORDERS RISE

The global COVID-19 pandemic has changed life as we knew it—and likely for the long haul. Going to school and work, restaurants, concerts, and sporting events might never be quite the same. Social distancing, face masks, and vaccines seem to have become the new normal. Many store shelves that were bare soon after the start of the pandemic are looking bare yet again. Businesses have had difficulty finding and keeping workers. Prices for many of the things we want and need are rising.

And that is not all. The pandemic and the ways in which it has changed people's lives continue to take a toll on mental health. Early on, people had to endure lockdowns, social isolation, shortages of food and supplies, the fear of getting ill, the worry of losing a loved one, and more. Even after restrictions were loosened, uncertainty about the long-term effects of COVID-19 on health and daily life kept anxiety high. Worries about the future continue to be widespread, since the virus keeps changing and disagreement about what needs to happen to help society get back to normal grows ever more emotional.

A Surge in Eating Disorders

The pandemic has brought about increased stress, depression, anxiety, and isolation. One result of these heightened emotions has been a surge in new cases and relapses of eating disorders—especially among teenagers and young adults.

Rory Monaco is one of them. The Connecticut college student developed an eating disorder during the pandemic. On a December 2020 evening, in the midst of the pandemic, Monaco's dad baked a pizza for the family. But when it came time to sit down to eat, Monaco could not take a single bite. A panic rose inside her that she could not control and did not quite understand. Monaco says, "The guilt you feel is literally like you just murdered someone. If I ate . . . I literally can't even explain it. I sobbed over eating a slice of pizza. . . . That sounds so absurd. And in the moment, you know it's absurd, but you also know that's the only way you're going to feel safe, and the only thing that's going to help your anxiety is to listen to your eating disorder."[1]

Peyton Crest, age eighteen, had an eating disorder before the pandemic. She thought she had it under control, but she relapsed twice during the pandemic. A junior in high school and getting ready to apply to colleges, she already felt anxious and under pressure. Then came the pandemic. Her classes went online, and people had to practice social distancing. All at once she could not see her friends and classmates. She lost her support system. She spent days by herself in her room, and all she could think about was food and how not to eat. She sought treatment for her eating disorder in June 2020 and thought the treatment had been successful. But then she relapsed again and spent two months in a residential treatment center. After treatment, Crest's school returned to in-person learning and she was accepted to college. Both of these events contributed to a big improvement in her mental health.

Before the pandemic, fifteen-year-old Amelia Haywood was happy and doing well in school. That changed when the lockdowns started. Haywood felt lost. "People are dying," she told a reporter. "Everyone's getting sick. You can't see your friends. It was hard because I felt like I didn't have any control over anything except what I ate and how I exercised."[2] Haywood was diagnosed with anorexia nervosa around February 2021, after visiting the emergency department four times and being admitted to the hospital three times in less than a year.

Sixteen-year-old Hannah grappled with an eating disorder before the pandemic. "There were huge readjustments and my eating disorder thrived off that and not seeing friends—at that time my anxiety took over," she says. She recalls how the pandemic caused her anxiety to go "up and down." She says, "I was sitting in front of the news and not knowing what the rules were going to be that week and getting your hopes up and then being disappointed . . . thinking you can get out but then you can't was really tough."[3]

The COVID-19 pandemic has brought increased stress, depression, anxiety, and isolation to many young people, leading to a surge in new cases and relapses of eating disorders.

Coping with a New Normal

Those who understand how and why eating disorders develop and progress are not surprised about the surge during the pandemic. The circumstances surrounding the pandemic laid a perfect foundation for eating disorders to develop or worsen. Disruptions in health care services, resulting from a system overloaded by severe COVID-19 cases, made getting care for eating disorders and other medical needs challenging. Now, as people struggle to get back to normal, eating disorders are not necessarily diminishing, and getting teenagers the care they need has not entirely improved.

There is still hope for people with eating disorders during this pandemic, though. They can take steps to get help and manage their disorder.

CHAPTER ONE

WHAT ARE EATING DISORDERS?

Many people worry about their weight or what their body looks like. They diet and try to eat healthy foods. They exercise to stay in shape and to lose or maintain their weight. Doctors, nutritionists, and other health care professionals agree that maintaining a healthy weight has several benefits. However, some people become overly concerned about their weight, food intake, and body image or shape. This obsession can progress into an eating disorder.

Eating disorders are serious and sometimes fatal illnesses in which people experience severe disturbances in their eating behaviors and have related thoughts and emotions. According to an article on the Yale Medicine website:

> For people with an eating disorder, weight is a critical part of their identity. If the number on the scale goes up, they feel humiliated. To prevent that from happening, they may restrict themselves to certain types of food and carefully balance what they eat with calorie-burning exercise. A gain of a pound or two may be punished by skipping the next meal. Then, when these restrictions become unsustainable, they might eat a couple of candy bars, but in secret, hiding the wrappers. And so begins a cycle that is hard to break.[4]

According to the National Eating Disorders Association, 20 million women and 10 million men have struggled with an eating disorder at some point in their lives. Ninety-five percent of people with eating disorders are ages twelve to twenty-five. *Eating disorders* is a general term. There are, in fact, several types of eating disorders. The most common are anorexia nervosa, bulimia nervosa, and binge-eating disorder. While they have their similarities, they also have distinct differences.

Anorexia Nervosa

Anorexia is probably the most familiar eating disorder. People with anorexia often consider themselves to be overweight even when they are very underweight. They typically weigh themselves several times a day, severely restrict the amount of food they eat,

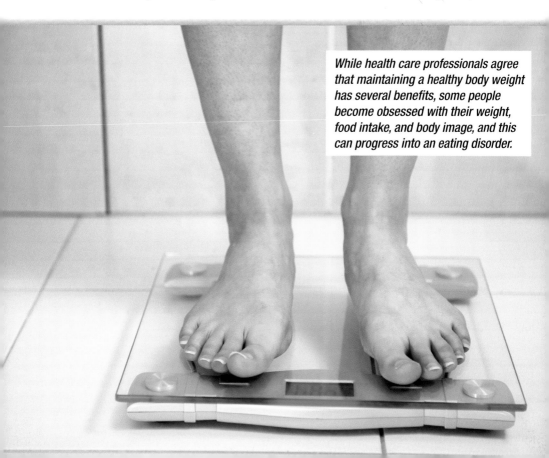

While health care professionals agree that maintaining a healthy body weight has several benefits, some people become obsessed with their weight, food intake, and body image, and this can progress into an eating disorder.

and often exercise excessively. Some with anorexia may force themselves to vomit and may use laxatives to lose weight. Laxatives are substances that loosen the stools and increase bowel movements.

Other signs and symptoms of anorexia include extreme thinness or emaciation, an insistent drive to be thin and unwillingness to maintain a healthy weight, intense fear of gaining weight, distorted body image, self-esteem heavily influenced by perceptions of body weight and shape, and/or denial of the seriousness of low body weight. According to the National Institute of Mental Health, anorexia nervosa has the highest death rate of any mental disorder. Many of these deaths are the result of complications associated with starvation. Suicide is also a risk.

People who struggle with anorexia all have similar symptoms, but each patient experiences the illness in his or her own way. Helena was diagnosed with anorexia nervosa when she was sixteen. She had been a healthy weight all her life, but she worried about her weight and what she looked like. She often compared herself to others and judged her own body harshly. Helena looked at herself in the mirror often and did not like what she saw. She hated that her thighs touched. She started her first weight loss diet when she was fourteen. She decided to become a vegetarian a year later and started to eliminate many foods. At fifteen Helena weighed 125 pounds (56.7 kg). By sixteen she had dropped down to 110 pounds (50 kg).

Even with the weight loss, Helena thought she weighed too much. She weighed herself several times a day and spent a lot of her time worrying about her weight. She dropped out of her normal activities and spent more and more time alone. She kept losing weight, too. Before she turned seventeen, she weighed 98 pounds (44.5 kg). Helena's parents were very concerned and took her to see her doctor. Based on the small amount of food she was eating, her low weight and heavy exercise, and her constant concern about her weight despite not weighing much, the doctor diagnosed her with anorexia nervosa.

Black People and Eating Disorders

Eating disorders have long been viewed as a problem that mostly affects young White females, but this is a misconception. Black teens, for example, are 50 percent more likely than White teens to exhibit bulimic behavior, according to the National Eating Disorders Association.

Anissa Gray is familiar with this problem. She is a senior editor at CNN Worldwide and author of the acclaimed novel *The Care and Feeding of Ravenously Hungry Girls*. Gray, who is Black, has battled bulimia and over-exercising for years. Early on, Gray did not think she had an eating disorder. "This little voice inside my head said: 'Black girls don't get eating disorders.'" She had never seen a Black woman talk openly about having an eating disorder.

This lack of exposure of Black people with eating disorders is why Gray decided to write a novel in which the main character has bulimia. "Eating disorders are largely seen as 'white girl problems,'" she says. "My story . . . shows that bulimia and anorexia are major issues for black girls, too. Talking and writing about this is, for me . . . a matter of life and death."

Anissa Gray, "It's Time to Correct the Narrative Surrounding Black Girls and Eating Disorders," Shondaland, January 2, 2020. www.shondaland.com.

While many people associate eating disorders with young girls, boys can struggle with their weight and body image, too. They also develop eating disorders. According to the National Eating Disorders Association, at least one-third of people with eating disorders are male. Some researchers say that number is probably even higher, because many go undiagnosed. Zach Schermele was diagnosed with anorexia at sixteen, but it took him a long time to accept it. He says:

> I have struggled with food and body image all my life. In fifth grade, I hid underneath a hotel bed for hours to evade being seen in a swimsuit by my own family. . . . By the time I was a sophomore in high school, I had been waging a silent war against sporadic "dieting" for years.[5]

In high school Zach joined the swim team, but he had to quit because his parents could no longer afford the membership fee. Then his dad switched jobs, and his brother told the family he was gay. The stress in their home was off the charts. Stress is often a factor in the elevation of eating disorders. Zach's disordered eating peaked during this time. "I vividly remember the day I trudged up another daunting flight of stairs at my high school . . . feeling only one emotion: pride. For three days and counting, I had somehow managed to subsist on barely eating anything. As a result, my head was clear, I felt thin, and it was all just difficult enough to keep me distracted from my family troubles."[6] Twenty-four hours later Zach was passed out on the living room floor. His parents were terrified. Soon Zach reluctantly entered treatment for his eating disorder.

Bulimia Nervosa

Bulimia nervosa is another eating disorder. People with bulimia go through cycles of bingeing and purging to undo the effects of the binge eating. When people binge eat, they consume a large amount of food in a short time. For many there is a sense of loss of control over what or how much they eat. Those who binge usually do so in secret and often feel ashamed or embarrassed. They often continue to consume food to the point of feeling sick to their stomach.

Following a bingeing episode, a person with bulimia will often purge, an unhealthy way to get rid of the calories they consumed during the binge. The goal of purging is to avoid gaining weight. The most common purging behavior is vomiting, but there are other methods, including overexercising, misusing laxatives or diuretics (water pills), and strict dieting.

Most people who binge eat do so weekly. As with anorexia, people with bulimia are consumed with thoughts of food and their body weight or shape. Often feeling bad about how they look, they have low self-esteem and self-worth. Unlike people with anorexia, however, those with bulimia may be normal weight, overweight,

People with bulimia often binge eat, then purge to undo the effects of the binge eating. Vomiting is the most common purging behavior.

or obese. Because they can be normal weight or overweight and they hide their eating behaviors, it can be difficult for others to recognize the problem.

Claire says her eating disorder started when she was fourteen years old. She watched a movie about a girl with an eating disorder

Other Underdiagnosed Groups

Eating disorders are most common in White females, but that does not mean they are not found in other populations. When it comes to eating disorders, boys and young men are often overlooked and underdiagnosed, because people simply think the disorders do not affect males. In fact, research suggests that males may account for up to half of all cases of eating disorders.

LGBTQ individuals are another underdiagnosed group. According to recent studies, eating disorders are more common among LGBTQ teenagers than other teens. Researchers believe this may be related to higher rates of body dissatisfaction, stigma, and victimization among these groups. Because these groups are often the target of bias and discrimination, they can be under a lot of stress, may be socially isolated, and often have negative thoughts about themselves. These factors often contribute to eating disorders.

and was fascinated by it. She was a bit overweight at the time and attending an all-girls school. Many of her schoolmates talked of vomiting after eating as a way to lose weight. Claire slowly became attracted to the idea of losing weight this way.

Purging seemed quick and easy—and it was. Claire did not particularly like the act of vomiting, but she liked how she felt afterward. "The first time I forced myself to be sick was unpleasant and upsetting but I remember the absolutely wonderful feeling of purity and emptiness following it. I had eaten an entirely normal meal and yet had eaten nothing at all!" Claire decided to stick with her new "weight loss method." She skipped breakfast and lunch, ate dinner, and promptly vomited. After four months of this routine, things got out of control. "The irony of bulimia," she says, "is that it starts out as a situation which is completely in the control of the person. However, it quickly snowballs and becomes a situation which is totally uncontrollable. My first binge terrified me because I had no control over it, the hunger was from deep within and was insatiable."[7]

Binge-Eating Disorder

Binge-eating disorder is another eating disorder in which people consume large amounts of food in a short period, experience a sense of loss of control over their eating, and then feel upset by their behavior. What makes this disorder different from bulimia nervosa is that individuals do not purge, or try to get rid of the food they ate by vomiting, fasting, overexercising, or misusing laxatives or water pills. Instead, they continue to binge eat, which can lead to serious health problems, including obesity, diabetes, high blood pressure, and heart disease.

Doctors give a diagnosis of binge-eating disorder when a person binges at least once a week for three months, feels a lack of control, and has three or more other signs and symptoms of the disorder. These include eating more rapidly than normal, eating until uncomfortably full, and eating large amounts of food when not hungry. Other signs include eating alone to hide feelings of shame over one's eating habits and experiencing disgust, depression, or guilt after bingeing.

Vanessa has experienced all of these sensations. Her binge-eating disorder was at its worst in her thirties, but she admits her troubles with food started when she was very young. "I've had issues with food for as long as I can remember," Vanessa says. "At around 10 years old, someone told me to stop eating because I'd get fat. From that moment, the war in my head started. I wanted to eat, but I also wanted to stop eating to avoid putting on weight. I started starving myself, which in turn led to more binge eating."[8]

> "At around 10 years old, someone told me to stop eating because I'd get fat. From that moment, the war in my head started. I wanted to eat, but I also wanted to stop eating to avoid putting on weight."[8]
>
> —Vanessa, a woman with a binge-eating disorder

Vanessa developed powerful cravings that she could not control. "Eating became an unconscious thing; it wasn't a lack of willpower, it was like I was on autopilot," she says. "When I was binge-eating, I would swear not to do it and the next minute I'd find myself stuffing food into my mouth. If someone had watched the process they would have seen me gulping down one thing after another." Vanessa felt powerless in the face of her disorder. "During a binge, I didn't even take the time to taste the food and it wasn't satisfying at all. After a binge, I would be consumed with guilt and shame. Binge eating takes over your whole life and thrives in isolation and shame."[9]

How Eating Disorders Affect the Body

Food provides the body's energy. The body uses this energy to do the work of keeping a person alive. This work is called metabolism. When the body is starved of food, or energy, for long periods, it adapts by slowing its metabolism and decreasing the amount of energy it needs. If a person continues to starve the body of food, the body is eventually unable to function properly. Organs may even shut down, ultimately leading to death.

Before that point, starvation and other behaviors may lead to a whole array of potentially dangerous health problems. Some—such as brittle hair and nails, dry and yellowish skin, and growth of fine hair all over the body (called lanugo)—are signs of illness, but they do not pose an immediate threat. Other effects present more serious risks. These include thinning of the bones, muscle wasting and weakness, severe constipation, low blood pressure, brain and heart damage, multiorgan failure, and a drop in internal body temperature.

Disordered Eating Is Complex

Anyone can develop an eating disorder. While many people associate eating disorders with females, males are at risk too. Overall, anorexia and bulimia are higher among females, but binge-eating disorder is more prevalent in males. Researchers reporting in the *International Journal of Eating Disorders* say that the differences between the genders depend on specific symptoms. For example, females are more likely to be unhappy with their weight, diet to control their weight, and purge while males are more likely to

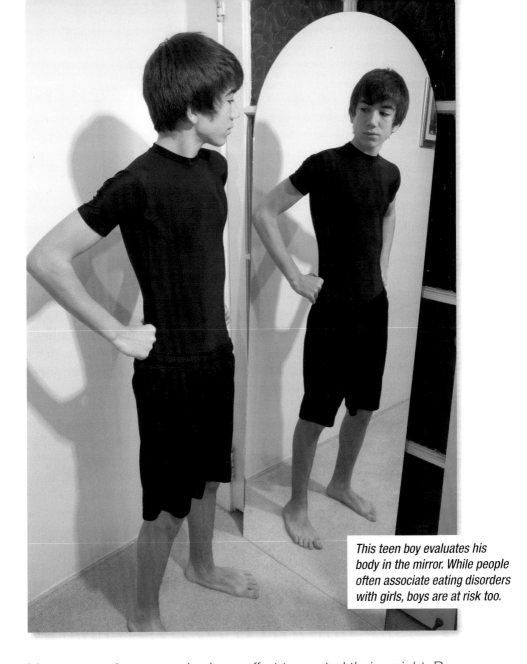

This teen boy evaluates his body in the mirror. While people often associate eating disorders with girls, boys are at risk too.

binge eat and overexercise in an effort to control their weight. Because many people assume males do not have eating disorders, they are often diagnosed later than females. Plus, males are less likely to seek treatment, which increases the chance of dying from their illness.

Many people are quick to look for simple causes for eating disorders. They want to blame the media's promotion of overly skinny models, or they point their finger at parents, claiming they must be doing something wrong. Research has shown over and over, however, that the root causes of disordered eating are way more complex.

The reality is that researchers cannot pinpoint one thing that causes a person to develop an eating disorder. Nor can they predict who might start disordered eating behaviors. Eating disorders are extremely complicated illnesses, and several elements play a role or contribute to their development and progression.

Anne Marie O'Melia is the chief medical officer and chief clinical officer at the Eating Recovery Center in Denver, Colorado. She believes eating disorders are "bio-psycho-social," meaning there are "genetics, psychological factors and social influences all at play"[10] in the development of eating disorders. Each person with an eating disorder, whether it be anorexia, bulimia, or binge-eating disorder, paves a unique path to the illness.

Risk Factors

Instead of *causes*, health care professionals often discuss *risk factors* for certain illnesses and disorders. A risk factor is not a direct cause, but instead is something that may increase the likelihood that a person will develop a disease or disorder. For example, having a close relative (a parent or sibling) with an eating disorder or mental health condition such as anxiety or depression is considered a risk factor for eating disorders.

Some of this risk is biological. One study of twins, for instance, found that 40 to 60 percent of the risk for the more common eating disorders may be connected to genetics. However, this does not mean that a certain gene or genes cause eating disorders. Instead, it is possible that people inherit traits such as anxiety, fear, and perfectionism, all of which can contribute to the development of an eating disorder.

According to the National Eating Disorders Association, a history of dieting is another risk factor, especially for binge eating.

Restrictive diets force the body to adjust to a calorie intake and eating regimen that is not optimal for physical health and wellness. This can foster the cycle of bingeing and purging or other unhealthy eating behaviors. In the extreme, dieting can become a way for people to exercise control when they feel their lives are out of control. The act of counting and restricting calories, limiting the types of and amounts of food one eats, and obsessing about the number on the scale can create a sense of control.

Several psychological risk factors also may play a role in the development of eating disorders. The most likely of these are anxiety, depression, low self-esteem, and trauma such as childhood sexual abuse. According to research, perfectionism and inflexibility are also risk factors associated with eating disorders, especially anorexia and bulimia. People who strive for perfection set unrealistic expectations for themselves—they want to be perfect no matter the cost. They do so to avoid feelings of shame and judgment. If they succeed, they mistakenly believe, then they can avoid or minimize those uncomfortable, painful feelings. In addition, many people with anorexia and bulimia say they were inflexible as children—they always followed the rules and believed there was only one right way to do things.

Social risk factors for eating disorders include society's pressure to be thin. The message that thinner is better comes across loud and clear—on television, in movies, in magazines, and on social media. Research shows that exposure to this message can increase a person's dissatisfaction with his or her body, which can lead to eating disorders by increasing the likelihood of dieting and restricting foods. Another social risk factor is being the target of teasing or bullying, especially about one's weight. In fact, 60 percent of people with eating disorders list bullying as a contributing factor.

While there are many thoughts and theories about what might lead someone to develop an eating disorder, there is no one specific cause that anyone can pinpoint. Eating disorders more than likely result from a combination of several factors.

CHAPTER TWO

WHY THE PANDEMIC TRIGGERED EATING DISORDERS

The COVID-19 pandemic brought many changes to everyday life, including face masks, social distancing, and debates over vaccines. The lockdowns, stay-at-home orders, and fear of the unknown caused tremendous amounts of stress, anxiety, and depression for just about everyone. Being a teenager is hard enough in normal times. But the pandemic dealt teenagers, for whom interacting with peers is key to their lives and development, an especially hard mental health blow.

Social Isolation

Early in the pandemic, schools closed their doors to in-person learning. Teenagers were suddenly cut off from seeing their peers and could no longer engage in after-school activities. People were encouraged to stay home and create a small bubble of people they could be with. For teenagers, that bubble typically included their immediate family members—no teachers, no friends, no counselors, no extended family, no teammates. They had to stay home and settle for social interaction via computer or phone screens. For many teenagers, this social isolation and the boredom it caused led to depression, anxiety, and other mental health challenges.

In 2019 an intervention program called Teen Mental Health First Aid was launched in one hundred US high schools with help from the Johns Hopkins Bloomberg School of Public Health. The goal of the program was to teach high school students how to identify and respond to signs of mental illness in their peers. The COVID-19 pandemic interfered with the program, as students turned to online learning in 2020. However, researchers from Johns Hopkins decided to ask some of the students questions about changes in their lives during the pandemic. Their survey sought to learn whether they were experiencing heightened stress or other problems stemming from those changes. "Well over 50% reported that the pandemic and response has created problems," says Holly Wilcox, a professor at the Bloomberg School of Public Health and one of the researchers. "A subset reported a 'great deal' or 'moderate' increase in depression (19% and 17%, respectively). We saw very large numbers report having changes in sleep and eating patterns."[11]

Most experts agree that the pandemic created a perfect scenario for the development or worsening of eating disorders among teenagers. David Little, a family physician who studied data surrounding eating disorder–related hospitalizations during the pandemic, found a definite spike. "The pandemic has been so disruptive to everyone's social interactions and to their own psychology," he said. "Teens are coming to grips with their vulnerability as humans and they are seeing suffering all around them. And there are, of course, the social aspects, no school, no in-person engagement with friends. That plays itself out in different ways."[12]

Fourteen-year-old Harriet developed anorexia nervosa during the pandemic. "I felt alone, bored and overwhelmed with school work" during the lockdown, she says. "I used my spare time to pick myself apart negatively."[13] Harriet's mother, Annette, says she would sit for an hour waiting for Harriet to eat. "I would give her a sandwich and she would pick it up, physically shake and then put it down."[14] Annette adds that even as her daughter's weight dropped, Harriet would still say she felt fat. By December

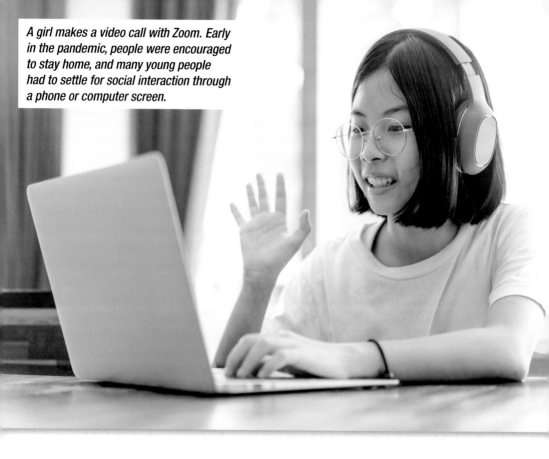

2020, Harriet started to have chest pains and was told she was at risk for a heart attack. Harriet was admitted to a treatment center where she could get help.

Rising Anxiety

For teenagers who were already battling an eating disorder, the pandemic and the shutdowns, isolation, and unknowns that came with it were especially difficult. After all, teenagers living with an eating disorder already deal with fear and panic on a daily—sometimes hourly—basis. The pandemic just piled on more. "We are in sort of an eating disorder crisis," pediatrician Nicole Hinkley-Hynes said in an October 2021 interview. "With the anxiety they [teenagers] feel about the world around them, they turn to things they can control including their diet and exercise."[15] In the first ten months of 2021, Hinkley-Hynes had seen a 25 to 30 percent increase in children referred to her hospital's eating disorder program.

Many statistics show that eating disorders have surged during the pandemic. Since the shutdowns began in early 2020, eating disorder support group memberships have increased, waiting lists for recovery treatment have lengthened, and hospitalizations for eating disorders have risen. More specifically, the National Eating Disorders Helpline experienced a 40 percent increase in calls during the first year of the pandemic. And throughout the pandemic, eating disorders remained the second-deadliest mental illness.

> "We are in sort of an eating disorder crisis. With the anxiety they [teenagers] feel about the world around them, they turn to things they can control including their diet and exercise."[15]
>
> —Nicole Hinkley-Hynes, pediatrician

Stress, Disruption, and Relapse

Considering the factors that can contribute to the development of eating disorders, including stress, depression, and anxiety, the increased incidence during the pandemic is not surprising. Researchers and health care professionals agree that several factors associated with the pandemic and the nature of eating disorders laid the groundwork for the rise. "Eating disorders are disorders of isolation that interfere with emotional and social development," says physician Anne Marie O'Melia. "The circumstances of the pandemic have placed kids at higher risk of developing and maintaining high-risk disordered eating behaviors."[16]

While some of the eating disorder diagnoses that have occurred during the pandemic were new cases, many individuals who had an existing eating disorder experienced a relapse. According to researchers reporting in the *Journal of Eating Disorders*, "Not surprisingly individuals with eating disorders have reported increased social isolation, rumination [obsessive thinking] about eating, feelings of anxiety and depression, and decreased feelings of control and social support during the Covid-19 pandemic."[17] And for those in the midst of treatment, the pandemic exacerbated their symptoms and made it difficult to continue with treatment.

When Healthy Eating Goes Too Far

During the pandemic, the media reported on ways to stay healthy and avoid catching the virus. In response, many people turned to restrictive or trendy diets in hopes of keeping the virus at bay. One of those trends is known as *clean eating*. Eating *clean* means avoiding processed or refined foods and limiting one's diet to foods such as fruits, vegetables, and legumes.

While this type of diet, in general, is healthy, it becomes another form of disordered eating when it turns into an obsession. "It often starts from a place of good intentions," says psychologist Ramani Durvasula, "with a person maintaining a healthy lifestyle or making changes to a more healthy lifestyle. Over time it becomes a bit more obsessional—with a rigid focus on types of ingredients, types of foods, quantities, and time of day things should be eaten."

Doctors call this newer eating disorder orthorexia. A person with orthorexia avoids foods that are not considered *clean* even though some of these foods are healthful. Someone with orthorexia might be overly concerned about the quality or source of foods they eat, avoid eating foods prepared by others, show signs of malnutrition due to eliminating whole food groups, and spend a lot of time researching foods and obsessing over food labels.

Quoted in Rachel Barclay. "Orthorexia: The New Eating Disorder You've Never Heard Of," Healthline, October 20, 2018. www.healthline.com.

Stress is often a trigger for eating disorders, and the pandemic stressed out just about everyone. But for people with an existing eating disorder, the stress magnified their symptoms—which is not unusual. According to social worker Greta Gleissner, "When individuals get stressed, they often act in impulsive ways because they do not know how to transform the stress into something productive. For people diagnosed with an eating disorder, these impulses from environmental and social stressors can cause individuals to not eat enough food, purge after a meal, or engage in a binge-eating episode."[18]

Among the many factors that can explain the rise in eating disorders during the pandemic, experts have focused on a few. One is the disruption of daily activities and the restrictions and lockdowns enforced early in the pandemic. This included restrictions on exercise and grocery shopping and the scarcity of certain foods. While hard on everyone, these were even more distressing for those with strict and inflexible exercise or eating patterns. Many individuals and families felt the need to stockpile food, which, for those with a tendency to binge eat, led to the very real risk of falling into a pattern of bingeing on those foods.

The changes to daily activities also led to a decrease in social supports, including access to treatment. With social distancing in place, face-to-face visits with therapists and other health care providers became impossible. What is more, many health care resources were redirected to address the management of COVID-19.

People stock up on food at an Oregon Costco in 2020. The COVID-19 pandemic caused many people to stockpile food; however, for those with a tendency to binge eat, this increased the risk of bingeing.

Too Much Screen Time

Another factor in the surge of eating disorders was the increased use of social media. Isolated from their friends and feeling bored, teens spent more time engaged with social media than before the pandemic. This resulted in more exposure to harmful eating and appearance-related content. That is in addition to the reality of stressful and traumatic world events that also negatively affect self-esteem and eating behaviors. O'Melia notes:

> Social media offers a constant way to compare yourself to others and to rely on superficial means of building self-esteem, such as how many "likes" or comments you get on a post. And unlike magazines or TV and movies, where even kids generally know there's a certain amount of professional make-up and editing happening, social media gives the impression that it's more "real," when it can be anything but. So young people are comparing themselves to an unrealistic and often impossible standard, which can lead to dangerous behaviors in an attempt to achieve something unachievable.[19]

During the pandemic, people did not just pay attention to their social media feeds, they also watched a lot of traditional media coverage. Stuck at home with little to do, watching the news was the only connection to the outside world some people had. Many wanted as much information as they could get about the virus, the pandemic, and what would happen next. For many, it was simply too hard to turn the TV off.

For teenagers with eating disorders stuck at home, though, some of the messages that came through the hours upon hours of media coverage were hard to take. For example, many news outlets did stories about the so-called quarantine 15, or the 15 pounds (6.8 kg) people thought they would gain due to eating more and exercising less during the lockdowns. And there was a focus on weight as a determining factor in hospitalizations related to COVID-19. More specifically, the heavier a person was, the more likely he or she was to be hospitalized and on a ventilator. Teens with eating disorders absorb messages like these, internalize them, and become even more worried, fearful, and obsessed with their own weight.

Pandemic Effects

When the lockdowns started, Cynthia Bulik, director of the University of North Carolina Center of Excellence for Eating Disorders, and Christine Peat, director of the National Center of Excellence for Eating Disorders, got to work to understand how the pandemic-related isolation was affecting people with eating disorders. The researchers surveyed approximately one thousand participants in the United States and Netherlands in April and May 2020. After getting some of the survey results, Bulik commented:

> People with eating disorders are really struggling. Those who are alone are really feeling the lack of support and are saying that they find themselves swirling around in negative thoughts. Many are also finding it hard to stay motivated to recover. On the other hand, some who are working on recovery, but are living in close quarters with others are having trouble finding the privacy to, for example, have telehealth sessions with their treatment team.[20]

Bulik and Peat found that US participants with anorexia nervosa reported they had increased their dietary restrictions and had fears about not being able to find foods they needed to follow their meal plans. And meal planning for people with eating disorders is crucial for their recovery. According to Lauren Muhlheim, a certified eating disorders expert, "Recovery from all

"People with eating disorders are really struggling. Those who are alone are really feeling the lack of support and are saying that they find themselves swirling around in negative thoughts."[20]

—Cynthia Bulik, director of the University of North Carolina Center of Excellence for Eating Disorders

Eating Disorders and COVID-19 Complications

People with underlying health conditions or a weakened immune system are at greater risk for suffering complications of COVID-19. Eating disorders can weaken the immune system, lead to extreme weight loss, and result in malnutrition. All of these conditions increase the likelihood of severe disease in people who are infected by the coronavirus.

Because the virus is still fairly new, additional research is needed to determine the risk of COVID-19 complications to people with eating disorders. However, a 2021 article in the *Journal of Eating Disorders* notes that early research suggests that people who are obese and have an eating disorder are at increased risk for getting a COVID-19 infection and suffering complications. This also holds true for severely malnourished patients with anorexia. With this in mind, experts recommend that people with eating disorders take extra care in following guidelines to avoid exposure to the virus.

eating disorders requires the normalization of regular eating patterns. Research has shown that this goal is best accomplished through planned and structured eating."[21]

The rise in eating disorders during the pandemic did not surprise J.D. Ouellette. Her seventeen-year-old daughter said she was starting what she called a "healthy eating makeover," which eventually became anorexia nervosa. She lost 25 percent of her body weight in three months. She has since recovered, and Ouellette now helps other parents of kids with eating disorders. Says Ouellette, "COVID plus lockdown created a perfect storm around anxiety, food scarcity messages, food access, and being home all the time, lack of structure, societal messaging on 'Quarantine 15,' more time to exercise, sometimes a family change or goal, depression leading to negative energy balance, and more."[22]

Heightened Focus on Food and Exercise

In June 2021, more than a year into the pandemic, health care professionals who treat patients with eating disorders attended the International Conference on Eating Disorders. The pandemic's effect on eating disorders dominated their conversations. Many attendees shared stories of how the lockdowns and lack of treatment options were affecting their patients.

Ellen Rome, head of adolescent medicine at Cleveland Clinic in Ohio, was one of the conference attendees. "At a consultation, kids tell us that when the pandemic started, they decided to eat healthier and begin exercising more," she said. "Then an adult will pick up the story and say, 'The next thing we knew, she'd lost [22 pounds].' Other kids tell us that without a schedule they started eating when they were stressed or bored and 'suddenly the weight balloons'"[23]

A young man exercises at home. During pandemic lockdowns, some young people developed an extreme and unhealthy focus on eating and exercise habits.

Amelia Haywood, who developed an eating disorder during the pandemic, is a case in point. Early in the pandemic, she established goals of eating a healthy diet and staying in shape. But as the shutdowns and isolation dragged on, her focus on food and exercise reached a new level. She tried new recipes, took pictures to post on Instagram, and then gave the food to her sister to eat. Amelia would lie and say she had already eaten. She would skip other activities to get in more exercise, usually a run. Soon she was losing weight, and it showed; she wore baggy clothing to cover it up. By the beginning of 2021, she felt drained and exhausted all the time.

The COVID-19 pandemic brought a lot of stress and anxiety. While everyone has had to learn to live with what has become "the new normal," the social isolation, loneliness, and changes in routines have hit teenagers especially hard. And many developed eating disorders as a way to cope.

CHAPTER THREE

GETTING TREATMENT

Treatment for eating disorders—during a pandemic or not—is complex. Most plans for recovery include nutrition counseling, psychotherapy (talk therapy), and sometimes medication. Each patient is different, so treatment must be tailored to the individual's specific needs. A patient and his or her treatment team need time to uncover and understand all the issues that contribute to the patient's disorder. But, experts say, time is of the essence. The longer an eating disorder continues, the more dangerous it becomes. In addition to addressing the disordered eating, treatment should include evaluating other health problems that already existed or were caused by the disorder. These conditions can be serious and even life threatening, especially if they have been ignored for too long.

People with eating disorders receive treatment either in an outpatient setting or as an inpatient in a hospital or treatment center. Which type of treatment a person receives depends on his or her physical and mental health. For example, if extreme weight loss is causing dehydration, sleeplessness, or other complications, doctors will probably recommend an inpatient treatment program. Likewise, inpatient treatment is common if the patient's mental state could lead to self-harm or if there is no progress with outpatient treatment. Outpatient treatment, on the other hand, is considered appropriate when the person's condition is relatively stable and continuous medical monitoring is not needed. Outpatient programs are less

expensive than inpatient programs. During the pandemic, with hospital beds in high demand, outpatient care has often been the only available option.

Nutrition Counseling

Nutrition counseling is a key component of treatment for eating disorders because the illness is not just about mental health. In treatment, patients learn the ways that disordered eating can damage their health. They also learn about the role nutrition plays in the healthy functioning of the body. As nutrition improves, physical health also improves, which in turn makes it more likely that people will respond to mental health counseling. James M. Greenblatt, a psychiatrist and chief medical officer of Walden Behavioral Care in Massachusetts, makes this point when he says, "I cannot overstate the importance of a sound nutritional program in the treatment of EDs [eating disorders]. . . . A nutritionally optimal environment makes recovery easier and plays a major role in the prevention of relapse. When the brain is receiving proper nourishment, symptoms may be relieved, and a patient will feel more motivated to participate in psychotherapy."[24]

The nutritionist often begins by identifying the patient's symptoms, attitudes, and beliefs surrounding food. Then the nutritionist offers support while providing nutrition education, helping the patient understand the difference between the myths and facts about food and nutrition. Throughout treatment, the nutritionist may assist the patient with symptom management, provide meal structure, assess and help improve the patient's recognition of hunger and fullness, and collect and monitor weight data.

Psychotherapy

To address the mental health component of eating disorders, cognitive behavioral therapy (CBT) is the most commonly used and recommended psychotherapy treatment. This version of talk therapy helps patients understand the connection between their thoughts, feelings, and behaviors and then develop strategies to change unhelpful thoughts and behaviors to improve their mood and everyday functioning. Patients in CBT spend time talking with a therapist and then have "homework" to do outside of sessions. For example, patients might keep a record of what they eat and their thoughts, feelings, and behaviors in connection with that meal or snack. Once they have established a pattern of regular eating, they might be asked to try foods they fear and report back about the experience.

CBT for eating disorders follows a structured program, often made up of a certain number of sessions. The patient and therapist set goals. At each session, the patient weighs in, talks with the therapist, reviews homework, discusses skills, and solves problems. Typically, CBT for eating disorders includes several components, such as keeping food records, creating meal plans, being exposed to foods the patient fears, weighing regularly, developing strategies to prevent binges and other disordered behaviors, and

A teen boy talks to a therapist. Cognitive behavioral therapy—which includes spending time talking with a therapist—is a common treatment for eating disorders.

more. The components a therapist chooses all depend on each patient's particular circumstances and needs.

While nutrition counseling and CBT are two components of treatment for eating disorders, research has shown that different treatments can be effective in helping people with eating disorders. CBT is not the only therapy available. There are also family-based therapies and group therapies. Some patients may need medication, hospitalization, or treatment in a residential setting. Each patient—with the help and support of a health care team— needs to find the treatment options that work best for his or her situation.

Seeking Help

Getting help for an eating disorder is crucial to recovery. But getting those who need it to seek help can be a challenge. People with eating disorders are not always up front and open about their habits around eating. Many of them hide the signs and symptoms. Research confirms that people with eating disorders often do not seek help. According to a 2019 study, only about half of more than thirty-six thousand US adults with eating disorders said they had sought any form of help. People may not seek treatment because they do not want to make a big deal out of their problem, perhaps because they are ashamed or are not ready to face that they have a problem or need help. Some may even be so sick from the illness that they are unable, physically or emotionally, to do what it takes to ask for help.

In many cases, family members need to take the lead and help a person with an eating disorder get help and find care providers. Because of their age, teenagers need a parent or guardian to assist in getting help and following through with treatment. In certain circumstances, a parent or guardian may have to force his or her child into treatment, especially if the condition has become life threatening. However, individuals who are over age eighteen cannot be forced into treatment unless they are considered a danger to themselves or others.

Research shows that the involvement of family members in the treatment of eating disorders can have a positive effect on the outcome. Parents, grandparents, guardians, aunts, uncles, siblings, and others can all encourage a teen to seek help. They also can provide support during treatment and serve as allies to both the child and the treatment team.

Along Came the Pandemic

Getting treatment for any mental health condition has become more difficult during the pandemic. But treatment for eating disorders has been especially hard, in part due to the increasing number of cases and in part to the unknowns around the coronavirus. Early in the pandemic, many health care providers had to focus on caring for COVID-19 patients, and many people stayed away from doctors' and therapists' offices and other health care facilities out of fear of catching the virus. In some places, stay-at-home orders kept people from going out for anything other than groceries. But the need for eating disorder treatment was high and growing, and the need continues.

The people who have needed help for eating disorders during the pandemic include new cases, those who relapsed due to circumstances surrounding the pandemic, and those who were already in treatment when the pandemic began. With no other options, many of them called on hotlines for help. In early 2022, the National Eating Disorders Association reported that their hotline had experienced a 107 percent increase in contacts since the beginning of the pandemic.

The steep increase in people seeking help for eating disorders did not come as a surprise to Janet Lydecker, director of child eating and weight initiatives for Yale University's Program for Obesity, Weight and Eating Research. "We expected that eating disorders would be more of a problem during the pandemic, especially when kids were staying home," she says. "They're stressed and lonely, and they have access to food, so we do see more binge-eating. And then they gain weight and are desperate to lose it, so we see more restrictive eating."[25]

Restoring Balance

Like a lot of high school students before the pandemic, fifteen-year-old Ella (not her real name) played sports, had friends, and went to school. These things gave her life balance. But then the pandemic came along, and she no longer had any of that. "I wanted to do something proactive to help me cope, so I turned to exercise," she explains. "I'd run almost every day. I went for bike rides and for hour-long walks."[26]

Ella's mom was happy to see her daughter engaging in what seemed like healthy habits. But soon she noticed that Ella was on edge if she was not exercising. "I couldn't stop. I don't know why. I just couldn't," Ella says. "At one point, I didn't even like exercise. I just felt like I had to do it."[27]

Ella's parents started to worry and searched for professional help. After several months Ella was finally able to see a specialist. Her weight loss did not meet the criteria of an emergency situation so the specialist decided to keep tabs on Ella until an inpatient bed opened up. In the meantime, Ella continued to overexercise, and months later her family doctor recommended she go the emergency room. She was admitted to a hospital within hours.

Fast-forward to today, Ella is doing much better. She is finishing high school and looking forward to college. She is also continuing her treatment. "[My doctor] assured me that full recovery is possible, but it can take time," Ella says. "We keep a week by week summary of all of my improvements, and looking back I definitely feel like I have come a long way. But there's still a way[s] to go."[28]

How to Reach Out

If you know someone struggling with an eating disorder—or even if you just suspect someone is experiencing a problem—there are ways to help. One way is to talk to the person. But that does not mean talking about food, how the person looks, or your suspicions of what might be going on. If it is a friend, eating disorders specialist Nooshin Kiankhooy suggests simply asking how he or she is doing. "Let's say we've . . . gone out to dinner. And I've noticed that there has been a really big shift in them," says Kiankhooy. "I may just kind of go through the meal and then maybe a few days later give them a call and say, hey, how's it going? You know, I noticed that you seemed really down." You can also bring up the pandemic and comment on how hard life has been for everyone over the past couple of years. See where the conversation goes, and, if it seems right, offer to listen and help your friend find professional treatment.

Quoted in *All Things Considered*, "Eating Disorders on the Rise After a Year of Uncertainty and Isolation," NPR, June 15, 2021. www.npr.org.

An Increase in Hospitalizations

The number of patients with eating disorders admitted to hospitals also increased over the course of the pandemic. Physician David Asch and other researchers reviewed trends in health care for eating disorders and other behavioral health conditions from January 1, 2018, to December 31, 2020. Their study, published in November 2021, included more than 3 million patients of all ages. They found that hospitalizations for eating disorders remained about the same until May 2020—not too long after the lockdowns, restrictions, and shutdowns started. At that point, the number of patients admitted to hospitals for eating disorders more than doubled.

In another study, researchers looked specifically at teenagers and young adults hospitalized for eating disorders before and after the pandemic started. From 2017 to 2019 the University of Michigan health system admitted an average of fifty-six patients ages ten to twenty-three per year. They found that 125 eating disorder–related patients in that age range were hospitalized in the health system during the first year of the pandemic. When the study ended in March 2021, the number of hospitalizations was still on the rise. Researchers believe that a delay in seeking care due to concerns around the pandemic may have helped fuel this increase.

One of the researchers involved in the study, physician Alana Otto, believes their study shows how hard the pandemic has been on adolescents with eating disorders. "Our study suggests that the negative mental health effects of the pandemic could be particularly profound among adolescents with eating disorders. But our data doesn't capture the entire picture. They could be really conservative estimates."[29] Because her study only included young people struggling with severe illness to the point of hospitalization, Otto says it is likely that many more teens and

> "Our study suggests that the negative mental health effects of the pandemic could be particularly profound among adolescents with eating disorders."[29]
>
> —Alana Otto, an adolescent medicine physician

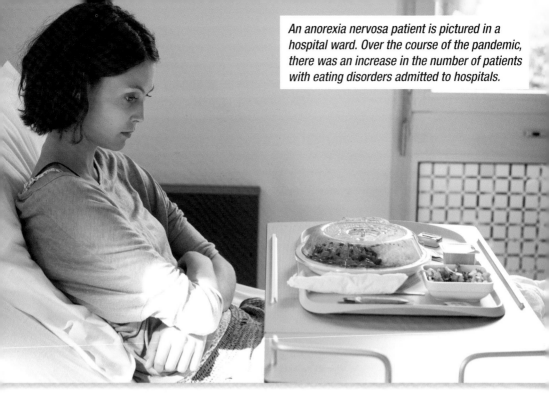

An anorexia nervosa patient is pictured in a hospital ward. Over the course of the pandemic, there was an increase in the number of patients with eating disorders admitted to hospitals.

young adults have been grappling with eating disorders brought on by the pandemic.

Facing the Increasing Demand for Help

In addition to hospitalizations, caregivers from dietitians to psychiatrists are having a tough time keeping up with the increasing demand for their services. Dana Greene, a dietitian who specializes in eating disorders, says she and her colleagues have done their best to help as many patients as possible but that many patients have had difficulty getting the treatment they need. In a November 2021 article, she said, "Eating disorders are through the roof. The resources are pretty tapped, so it's almost impossible to find help."[30]

In some cases patients who delayed getting treatment because of the pandemic have been in more advanced stages of the disorder once they finally started (or restarted) treatment. "We're seeing [that] not only are more people calling, but more people are calling in a more crisis situation,"[31] Jillian Lampert of The Emily Program said in 2020. Lampert's eating disorders program at the University of

Celebrities Open Up About Eating Disorders

Many teens look up to celebrities. So hearing that a celebrity has grappled with an eating disorder can help young people struggling with their own eating disorders find the courage to talk about it and seek help.

In January 2021 Taylor Swift talked about her struggles with an eating disorder in her documentary *Miss Americana*. Like most celebrities, Swift has to endure unsolicited criticism from fans, critics, and others about her looks and body shape. Because of that, she says, she has a hard time looking at pictures of herself every day, because they can trigger her eating disorder. Sometimes, she says, she would look at paparazzi pictures and see one where "I looked like my tummy was too big, or . . . someone said that I looked pregnant . . . and that'll just trigger me to just starve a little bit—just stop eating." She remembers a particular trigger when she was eighteen. A tabloid suggested that Swift looked pregnant on the cover of a magazine—her very first magazine cover.

Swift is not the only celebrity who has spoken openly about her eating disorder. Others include Demi Lovato, Lady Gaga, Zayn Malik, and Elton John.

Quoted in Marianne Garvey, "Taylor Swift Shares She Struggled with an Eating Disorder," CNN, January 24, 2020. www.cnn.com.

Minnesota has seen its daily calls for treatment double, from about 60 calls a day in 2019 to 130 a day since the start of the pandemic.

The rising number of adolescents with eating disorders has been particularly noticeable, says Katherine Ort, codirector of the KiDS of NYU Integrated Behavioral Health Program. "We are seeing a skyrocketing of adolescents coming in with eating disorders, and the increase is in both volume and severity," says Ort. She notes that recognizing the signs of an eating disorder early and getting help before the illness spirals out of control is essential. "The longer someone struggles, the harder it becomes to treat the eating disorder."[32]

But the circumstances surrounding the pandemic made getting help earlier very difficult. Jennifer Wildes, an associate psychiatry professor and director of an outpatient eating disorders program at the University of Chicago Medicine, says some patients have had to wait four to five months for treatment, including therapy and medication. Before the pandemic, most patients only had to wait a few weeks before getting help. Wildes's own eating disorders program has seen its caseload double since the pandemic began. Today caseworkers are treating about one hundred patients.

> "The longer someone struggles, the harder it becomes to treat the eating disorder."[32]
>
> —Katherine Ort, codirector of the KiDS of NYU Integrated Behavioral Health Program

Turning On Virtual Therapy

Eating disorders are one of the most difficult mental health disorders to treat under normal circumstances. They are even more of a challenge to manage during a crisis like the COVID-19 pandemic. Even before the pandemic, therapists and specialists who treat eating disorders were in high demand and short supply. The pandemic just made this worse. Doctors say parents have shared with them that they have had to call twenty, thirty, or more therapists and still could not find one who had openings to see their child.

Many mental health and other care providers had to figure out a way to help patients they could not see in person. Just as schools and workplaces went online, therapists, doctors, and other health care providers switched to videoconferencing and visits by phone. This care is known as teletherapy or telehealth. While teletherapy was a lifesaver for many, therapists and patients alike needed time to adjust to this new way of doing things.

Past research has shown that teletherapy services are effective for the treatment of mental health disorders. In fact, its effects can be equal to more traditional in-person therapy for specific mental health problems. However, research before the pandemic had not yet shown its effectiveness in treating eating disorders. This is partly because eating disorders treatment relies in part on in-person contact. Often a weigh-in is involved, and in-person monitoring of the patient's mental and physical health status is key. Visual cues, such as body language or facial expressions, often help guide sessions. All these are more difficult to obtain and assess over a screen. Still, early studies have shown that teletherapy could be beneficial for treating eating disorders.

In their study of how people with eating disorders coped with isolation related to the pandemic, Cynthia Bulik and Christine Peat found that more than 80 percent of those in treatment before the pandemic turned to teletherapy when in-person therapy was not an option. The researchers followed up with study participants each month, and many said they were satisfied with the care they received.

What Does the Future Hold?

Will this increased demand for eating disorders treatment continue? More than two years into the pandemic, it is hard to say. Some health care providers hope that life returning to some sense of normalcy will help improve the situation—that teens and young adults will get back to their regular routines, including those related to food. But as the world has learned over the past couple of years, life can change in an instant. Uncertainty about the future may be the one constant—and that is one of the stressors that can lead to or magnify eating disorders. Physician Caroline Carney says, "I think that eating disorders are a growing trend, and there to stay largely because of social media influences and the stressors brought on by the pandemic."[33]

Other health care providers believe the pandemic may have exposed the eating disorder problem that already existed among the young population. "I'm not convinced it's a growing trend," says Allison Chase, clinical director at the Eating Recovery Center, "but rather one that has existed, meaning that there has been disordered eating in our communities and often at a higher level. We're just seeing it more now, as the shift in environment exacerbated the physical symptoms."[34]

CHAPTER FOUR

COPING WITH AN EATING DISORDER DURING A PANDEMIC

People around the world have a seemingly infinite variety of stories to tell about how they have been coping with the COVID-19 pandemic. Some have described the heartbreaking loss of loved ones or how they overcame the virus themselves. Others have shared stories of feeling isolated, missing important family occasions such as graduations and weddings, losing a job, facing the fear and frustration of working in a high-risk setting, and coping with online school or working from home.

Then there are the stories that, on the surface, seem less dire. These are stories about weight gain, altered or abandoned exercise routines when gyms closed, and the inability to find certain foods on grocery store shelves as supply chain issues arose. While many people can bounce back from these types of challenges, many others cannot. The latter group includes people who have developed eating disorders or whose eating disorders relapsed during the pandemic. Their stories are not about experiencing minor inconveniences. Their stories are about the challenges of coping, seeking help, and hoping one day to lead a healthy, normal life.

Heather Loeb has her own story about coping with an eating disorder during the pandemic. She has struggled with anxiety,

Many gyms, such as this one, temporarily closed down during the COVID-19 pandemic. For people with eating disorders, changes in routine, such as the inability to workout at the gym, can make the eating disorder worse.

CLOSED

DUE TO COVID 19

CORONAVIRUS

depression, a binge-eating disorder, and other mental health conditions since middle school. She writes a blog called *Unruly Neurons*, where she shares her challenges and triumphs. Her eating disorder relapsed during the pandemic. "I have struggled greatly to control it [my binge-eating disorder]," she admits. "It's been my go-to coping mechanism for more than a decade. My disordered eating is triggered by stress and anxiety, which has been plentiful in the past year and half. Obviously I'm not alone."[35]

Loeb is nowhere near alone in her struggles with an eating disorder in the midst of a worldwide pandemic. And the personal stories of eating disorders continue to grow as the pandemic drags on. While everyone has had to endure changes, obstacles, annoyances, and feelings of isolation and despair, people with new or existing eating disorders continue to face special challenges.

Restrictions and Changes in Routines

People with eating disorders strive for routine—and the pandemic upended most people's routines. Teenagers experienced these changes in a way that others did not. For many months they could not go to school, see their friends, play team sports, or do other after-school activities. In a study of about 450 young patients admitted to the Royal Children's Hospital eating disorders treatment center in Melbourne, Australia, researchers found pandemic restrictions played a big role in their eating disorders. According to the data, about a fourth of patients surveyed reported that changes to their routines contributed to their eating disorder.

Loeb can relate to that. She knows that stress, isolation, social media use, and changes in interactions with friends and family have contributed to her own problems with eating disorders. She notes that the uncertainty of life during the pandemic, along with so many forced changes in her usual routines, have triggered her bingeing behaviors. As she explains:

> My anxiety forces me to plan ahead, and I just can't do that right now. Nobody can. I need structure to feel in control and maintain my mental health, and I'm not getting it. So when I feel like I've lost control, I turn to eating. I swallow my feelings and chase that high I get when I taste something, anything. And while I'm aware this isn't healthy, sometimes I can't help it, It's a compulsion. Eating disorders aren't a choice we make; they are mental disorders.[36]

Experts confirm that loss of structure and routine present considerable challenges to individuals who suffer from eating disorders. According to Christine Peat, who coauthored a study of eating disorders during the pandemic with Cynthia Bulik, "Many people in our study . . . were talking about concerns that their eating disorder would get worse because of a lack of structure a lack of social support. . . . And now that sense of structure has just kind of gone out the window. And with that can go the structure you had around your meals and your snacks."[37]

In Peat and Bulik's research, people with bulimia and binge-eating disorder reported increases in binge-eating episodes and greater urges to binge. Some also voiced their concern about living in a triggering environment during a pandemic. Says Bulik:

> We know that eating disorders thrive in isolation, and having social support can deter individuals with eating disorders from engaging in health-damaging behaviors, like excessive exercise, restriction, or purging. When you're alone, like during the pandemic, there are no social deterrents, so the eating disorder can escalate unchecked. That is why reaching out and staying connected is so important even if it is virtually, especially as the pandemic continues to drag on.[38]

Shopping for Food

The COVID-19 pandemic brought more changes that people did not anticipate. One of those changes concerned getting food. In the beginning of the pandemic, grocery shopping—once a routine chore for most—became much more difficult and complicated. At the time, people were afraid to be around others in public places—and with good reason. They knew little about the virus, including how it spread, and fears of catching the virus out in public ran high.

Soon, some foods were in limited supply, and stores created strict rules for shoppers. For example, stores asked families to send just one family member on shopping trips to help minimize the number of people in the store. Stores also restricted how many people could be in the store at a time. This often led to long lines and wait times to enter stores. Shortages of certain foods and supplies caused many stores to limit how many of a particular item one person could purchase.

Shortages also resulted in panic shopping. When they could, people stocked up on foods and other products that were in short supply or rumored to become scarce soon. At times this made shortages even worse and often left store shelves bare. Shoppers

Tips for Managing Recovery

In addition to treatment, there are things teens dealing with an eating disorder can do to help manage their illness. These tips can help bridge the time between seeking help and getting a treatment plan together.

While it is difficult for anyone with an eating disorder to reach out for help, during the pandemic—with the isolation, ever-changing rules, food challenges, and unknowns—it is more important than ever to seek support. Teens can start by connecting with people with whom they feel comfortable and can trust, such as a family member, friend, support group, or therapist.

Young people should limit the amount of time they spend checking social media and news feeds. It is also a good idea to unfollow any accounts that trigger anxieties or negative feelings.

Teens can also get help through free online or phone-based resources. Online support groups and social media feeds can help teens manage their eating disorder concerns. For example, the National Eating Disorders Association posts Facebook Live videos designed to help people cope with specific issues and topics.

needed to be creative and flexible in their search for food. When they could not find something, they had to hunt for something else to take its place.

Shopping is typically stressful for people with eating disorders. Each day and all day, food is on top of their minds as they contemplate rules about what, when, and how much they should eat. The sheer number of food products and labels they face when they walk through a store's doors is overwhelming and can cause anxiety, fear, and outright panic. For example, a person with binge-eating disorder may give into impulses, buying too much and eating it all in one binge episode.

The pandemic-related food shortages, along with the many rules and restrictions, made food shopping downright terrifying

A couple is pictured in a grocery store that has empty shelves as a result of COVID-19-related shortages. Shortages and restrictions caused by the pandemic made grocery shopping a stressful experience for some people with eating disorders.

for those with an eating disorder. As an example, many people with eating disorders need shopping support, a friend or family member to accompany them and help them navigate the aisles. The support person can help them stick to their grocery list or run interference against the urge to obsessively compare food labels or fill the cart with more than they need. But with the one-person-per-household rule in force, people with eating disorders were faced with shopping alone.

Francesca, age 21, says her biggest challenge during the pandemic was shopping for food. She was diagnosed with anorexia before the pandemic began—when she was just 16—and she had been through treatment. But as the crisis grew, her symptoms started to kick in again. She was one who relied on someone to accompany her when she shopped for groceries. She admits that other shoppers and grocery clerks did not recognize her as someone who would need that emotional support. "Some individuals may look absolutely fine on the outside," Francesca says, "but actually really need someone else to go shopping with them."[39]

Francesca explains that she needs structure and certainties in her life. She likes to get outside, go to the gym, and spend time with other people. But the pandemic lockdowns robbed her of those things. And that is when disordered eating can take over. Even though she was struggling with all the constant unknowns and changes, she worked hard to remain positive.

Dealing with Other Mental Health Disorders

Staying positive can be hard when faced with mental health challenges that go beyond eating disorders. And this is not uncommon, since many people with eating disorders also suffer from anxiety, depression, obsessive-compulsive disorder (OCD), or substance abuse disorder. According to one study, 97 percent of nearly twenty-five hundred female patients in treatment for an eating disorder were also diagnosed with one or more other mental health disorders. The most common were depression and anxiety disorder.

Eating disorder symptoms are often magnified by these other disorders. For example, a common symptom of anorexia nervosa is overwhelming concern about one's weight or body shape. Anxiety can increase the intensity of that concern. And some behaviors often seen in people with eating disorders are similar to the signs of OCD. People who struggle with OCD are very concerned or obsessed that things be exact and in order. They do not like to make mistakes. They follow a strict routine. In a similar way, people with eating disorders are often perfectionists, wanting to be exact with what foods they eat and when. According to researcher Anna-Rita Atti, OCD affects nearly 15 percent of patients who have an eating disorder.

The pandemic has caused some people with eating disorders and other mental health conditions to face new challenges. Stephanie Parker has struggled with eating disorders, anxiety, and OCD since childhood. The pandemic triggered those familiar and uncomfortable behaviors and feelings. Parker recalls, "The OCD and anxiety . . . just made my eating disorder more intense, and for me that meant I would become obsessed with cleaning everything and then checking in with myself to see if I deserve to eat. I would become scared of food—I got scared that food would make me sick because it wasn't clean enough."[40]

Mixed Views of Teletherapy

In an effort to cope with their eating disorders during the pandemic, many people actually have sought help. Because of restrictions on in-person counseling sessions, much of that help has come through teletherapy. Interviews with therapists and patients show mixed results.

Many therapists who were not sure how their patients would do with teletherapy have been surprised to find that connecting with patients online can be effective. Deborah Glasofer, a professor of clinical psychology at Columbia University Irving Medical Center, says, "If there is a silver lining, it is that therapists have expanded their use of teletherapy and are coming up with creative solutions to adapt treatments to an online format."[41]

As an example, some patients have a difficult time feeling comfortable seeing their body on camera. This is not surprising, considering that one of the symptoms of eating disorders is poor body image. Therapists have found ways to address this problem. They may have patients move back from the camera or use settings to minimize their on-screen image. Some therapists have even used the problem as a springboard to discuss the patients' negative feelings about their bodies.

In addition, some therapists have found that they can adapt their strategies to teletherapy sessions. For ex-

> "If there is a silver lining, it is that therapists have expanded their use of teletherapy and are coming up with creative solutions to adapt treatments to an online format."[41]
>
> —Deborah Glasofer, a professor of clinical psychology at Columbia University Irving Medical Center

During the pandemic, restrictions on in-person counselling meant that many patients had to use teletherapy instead. While some people liked this option, others found it much less effective than speaking to a therapist face to face.

ample, some have offered virtual sessions to discuss food preparation and meals; others have used screen sharing to help their patients fill a grocery cart or brainstorm alternative foods through an online food-delivery service.

Not all patients have had a favorable response to teletherapy, however. In a survey of patients with eating disorders, 74 percent of respondents who had moved from in-person sessions to teletherapy during the pandemic did not feel it was as effective. Anne, a patient with an eating disorder, says, "It became so easy to hide . . . all that my treatment team could see was my face so I would throw away certain parts of my meal or go to the bathroom immediately after the session."[42] Anne's revelation helps demonstrate why in-person therapy is so critical to treatment. Part of treatment for an eating disorder may include having the patient eat a meal in the presence of a care

Surviving with Support

According to surveys of people with eating disorders, spending time with family during the pandemic improved their bonds. And in some cases, those bonds helped family members become more supportive as communication and understanding improved.

This is good news because support from others is crucial to eating disorder recovery. Eric Dorsa has struggled with an eating disorder for years and is now a recovery advocate. Because of his history, Dorsa could relate to the stress many felt when foods became scarce during the pandemic. However, instead of resorting to old habits of restricting or bingeing, he connected with loved ones for support. "The most important thing is finding ways to connect with people that know you . . . that you feel you can open up to about where you're struggling."

Quoted in Megan Ball, "Coping with an Eating Disorder During the COVID-19 Pandemic," KENS5, September 19, 2020. www.kens5.com.

provider. That way, the patient is encouraged to finish the meal or eat foods that might cause fear and anxiety. In an in-person office setting, the patient cannot throw away foods or immediately purge. But, as Anne explains, these "secret" behaviors are easier to get away with in teletherapy.

Help from Friends

Those who have been forced to face their eating disorders alone during the pandemic have likely suffered more than those who have found support. Support can come in many forms. Banmai Huynh, a college student from Massachusetts, learned this when her friends convinced her to get help for an eating disorder that developed during the pandemic. With their encouragement, she started seeing a nutritionist, who helped her "realize that I deserve to nourish myself and food is not the enemy,"[43] she says.

Like many others, when the lockdowns began, Huynh wanted to keep her weight in check and her body healthy. But she went too far. She describes herself as getting caught up in diet culture. According to body image researcher Nadia Craddock, "Diet culture is that collective set of social expectations telling us that there's one way to be and one way to look and one way to eat and that we are a better person, we're a more worthy person if our bodies are a certain way."[44]

Huynh describes how, over the course of the pandemic, she became more and more obsessed with her weight and diet. She weighed herself constantly, always hoping to see the number on the scale go down. When that did not happen, she stopped eating. Her weight fell, but she was not any happier. "I hid my body with hoodies and sweats in 90 degree weather and I would constantly stand in front of the mirror criticizing every curve, dimple, or blemish I had," she says. "I relentlessly compared myself to unrealistic expectations, like Instagram influencers and supermodels, because I couldn't accept my body for what it was."[45]

Huynh is recovering from her eating disorder. For that she credits her friends, her family, and the mental health professionals who have all supported her efforts to develop a healthy view of food, weight, and her own body.

Unique Challenges

The pandemic has not been easy on anyone, but people struggling with an eating disorder have faced a unique set of challenges. Activities that are easy and perhaps mundane to most—such as sitting down to eat a meal or grocery shopping—can cause a lot stress and anxiety in people with eating disorders. This was perhaps even more evident for teenagers with eating disorders, as they had to face isolation from their peers and a lack of the structure they had become used to.

The good news is people with eating disorders—including teenagers—can get better. But diagnosing the problem and getting treatment as soon as possible are crucial to recovery. It is no exaggeration to say that getting help and taking steps to manage the disorder can save lives and help avoid serious medical complications. Unfortunately many people with eating disorders are in denial, feel guilty or ashamed, and hide their problem. "I still have a long road to recovery," says Huynh, "but when we normalize talking about mental health issues, we make people feel less embarrassed about their struggles and we encourage more people to share their stories and seek out the help they need."[46]

SOURCE NOTES

Introduction: As a Pandemic Rages, Eating Disorders Rise

1. Quoted in Alison Cross, "'I Sobbed over Eating a Slice of Pizza': Pandemic Fuels Increase in Eating Disorders," Connecticut Health I-Team, July 29, 2021. http://c-hit.org.
2. Quoted in Kate Wells, "Children's Hospitals Saw Rise in Eating Disorder Cases During Pandemic," *Weekend Edition Sunday*, NPR, August 8, 2021. www.npr.org.
3. Quoted in Nick Triggle, "Eating Disorders: The Terrible Impact of the Pandemic on the Young," BBC, July 22, 2021. www.bbc.com.

Chapter One: What Are Eating Disorders?

4. Quoted in Kathy Katella, "Eating Disorders on the Rise After Our Pandemic Year," Yale Medicine, June 15, 2021. www.yalemedicine.org.
5. Zach Schermele, "What No One Tells You About Being a Teenage Boy with Anorexia," HuffPost, October 2, 2018. www.huffpost.com.
6. Schermele, "What No One Tells You About Being a Teenage Boy with Anorexia."
7. Claire, "Claire's Story," Bodywhys, 2022. www.bodywhys.ie.
8. Vanessa, "Reflecting on My Binge Eating Disorder," SANE Australia, February 12, 2018. www.sane.org.
9. Vanessa, "Reflecting on My Binge Eating Disorder."
10. Quoted in Carly Menker, "Pandemic Fuels Rise in Eating Disorders Among Adolescents," American Academy of Pediatrics, June 1, 2021. https://publications.aap.org.

Chapter Two: Why the Pandemic Triggered Eating Disorders

11. Quoted in Jackie Powder, "Teen Mental Health During Covid-19," Johns Hopkins Bloomberg School of Public Health, May 17, 2021. https://publichealth.jhu.edu.
12. Quoted in Jamie Reno, "Eating Disorders Among Teens Have Risen During COVID-19: What Parents Can Do," Healthline, May 16, 2021. www.healthline.com.
13. Quoted in BBC, "Covid-19: Teen with Anorexia 'Overwhelmed' in Lockdown," March 3, 2021. www.bbc.com.

14. Quoted in BBC, "Covid-19."
15. Quoted in Katherine Cook, "Eating Disorders Increase Among Kids, Teens During Pandemic," KGW8 News, October 26, 2021. www .kgw.com.
16. Quoted in Menker, "Pandemic Fuels Rise in Eating Disorders Among Adolescents."
17. Rebecca Spigel et al., "Access to Care and Worsening Eating Disorder Symptomatology in Youth During the COVID-19 Pandemic," *Journal of Eating Disorders* 9, no. 1 (2021). www.ncbi.nlm.nih.gov.
18. Greta Gleissner, "Eating Disorders and Stress," *Hope for Eating Disorder Recovery* (blog), *Psychology Today*, January 30, 2017. www .psychologytoday.com.
19. Quoted in Menker, "Pandemic Fuels Rise in Eating Disorders Among Adolescents."
20. Quoted in UNC Health, "Researchers Collaborate to Study Pandemic's Impact on People with Eating Disorders," University of North Carolina at Chapel Hill, June 15, 2020. www.unc.edu.
21. Lauren Muhlheim, "Meal Planning for Eating Disorder Recovery," Verywell Mind, September 29, 2020. www.verywellmind.com.
22. Quoted in Reno, "Eating Disorders Among Teens Have Risen During COVID-19."
23. Quoted in Jane Feinmann, "Eating Disorders During the COVID-19 Pandemic," *British Medical Journal* 374, no. 1787 (2021). www .bmj.com.

Chapter Three: Getting Treatment

24. Quoted in Jessica R. Green, *Eating Disorders: The Ultimate Teen Guide*. Lanham, MD: Rowman & Littlefield, 2014.
25. Quoted in Katella, "Eating Disorders on the Rise After Our Pandemic Year."
26. Quoted in Sandee LaMotte, "'I Couldn't Stop.' The Pandemic Is Triggering Eating Disorders in Our Children," WTHI-TV, February 4, 2022. www.wthitv.com.
27. Quoted in Sandee LaMotte, "'I Couldn't Stop.'"
28. Quoted in Sandee LaMotte, "'I Couldn't Stop.'"
29. Quoted in Robert Preidt, "Teens Hospitalized with Eating Disorders Rose During Pandemic," WebMD, July 13. 2021. www.webmd.com.
30. Quoted in Denise Mann, "Study: Pandemic Doubled Need for Inpatient Care of Eating Disorders," UPI, November 25, 2021. www .upi.com.

31. Quoted in Katie Kindelan and Lauren Joseph, "Eating Disorder Hospitalizations Doubled During COVID-19 Pandemic, New Data Shows," ABC News, November 16, 2021. https://abcnews.go.com.
32. Quoted in Mann, "Study."
33. Quoted in Sofia Quaglia, "Study Finds Hospitalizations for Eating Disorders Doubled During the Pandemic," Verywell Health, November 29, 2021. www.verywellhealth.com.
34. Quoted in Quaglia, "Study Finds Hospitalizations for Eating Disorders Doubled During the Pandemic."

Chapter Four: Coping with an Eating Disorder During a Pandemic

35. Heather Loeb, "Mental Health Matters: Hospitalizations for Eating Disorders Have Doubled During Pandemic," Yahoo! News, January 17, 2022. https://news.yahoo.com.
36. Loeb, "Mental Health Matters."
37. Quoted in Noguchi, "Eating Disorders Thrive in Anxious Times, and Pose a Lethal Threat," NPR, September 8, 2020, ww.npr.org.
38. Quoted in National Institute of Mental Health, "Let's Talk About Eating Disorders with NIMH Grantee Dr. Cynthia Bulik," February 25, 2021. www.nimh.nih.gov.
39. Quoted in George Herd, "Covid, Mental Health and Your Lockdown Stories," BBC, February 27, 2021. www.bbc.com.
40. Quoted in Noguchi, "Eating Disorders Thrive in Anxious Times, and Pose a Lethal Threat."
41. Quoted in Carla Cantor, "Managing Eating Disorders During COVID-19," Columbia News, August 6, 2020. https://news.columbia.edu.
42. Quoted in William A. Haseltine, "How the Pandemic Is Fueling Eating Disorders in Young People," *Forbes*, August 27, 2021. www.forbes.com.
43. Banmai Huynh, "My Eating Disorder Recovery," Her Campus, January 28, 2022. www.hercampus.com.
44. Quoted in Andee Tagle and Clare Marie Schneider, "Diet Culture Is Everywhere. Here's How to Fight It," *Life Kit*, NPR, January 4, 2022. www.npr.org.
45. Huynh, "My Eating Disorder Recovery."
46. Huynh, "My Eating Disorder Recovery."

Eating Disorders Anonymous (EDA)

https://eatingdisordersanonymous.org

According to its website, the EDA is a group of people who share their experiences with one another with the goal of helping others recover from eating disorders.

Eating Disorders Coalition (EDC)

www.eatingdisorderscoalition.org

The EDC's goal is to raise awareness about eating disorders as a public health priority. Its website offers facts and other information about eating disorders and ways that individuals can get involved to help the coalition reach its goals.

The Emily Program

www.emilyprogram.com

This foundation provides support for people with eating disorders and raises community awareness of these conditions. The group also makes sure that people with eating disorders and their families receive the support they need.

National Alliance for Eating Disorders

www.allianceforeatingdisorders.com

This group provides referrals, education, and support for all eating disorders. Its goal is to raise awareness, eliminate secrecy and stigma, and promote access to care and support for people who are at risk for or currently experiencing and/or recovering from eating disorders.

National Association of Anorexia Nervosa and Associated Disorders (ANAD)

https://anad.org

Hotline: (888) 375-7767

ANAD provides free peer-support services to anyone who is struggling with an eating disorder. Volunteers who understand eating disorders and what it is like to go through treatment and recovery are ready to help others on their journey. The ANAD hotline is available Monday through Friday.

National Eating Disorders Association (NEDA)
www.nationaleatingdisorders.org
Helpline: (800) 931-2237 (call or text)
The NEDA is devoted to preventing eating disorders, providing treatment referrals, and increasing the education and understanding of eating disorders, weight, and body image. The association offers programs and services to support people with eating disorders and their families. The helpline is available Monday through Friday.

National Institute of Mental Health (NIMH)
www.nimh.nih.gov
The NIMH raises awareness and offers education to people affected by mental health disorders, including eating disorders. Visit the website to learn more about different eating disorders, their symptoms, and how they are treated.

UCLA Eating Disorders Program
www.uclahealth.org/eatingdisorders
This program provides treatment services tailored to the individual needs of children, adolescents, and adults with eating disorders. Health care providers treat the physical, mental, and emotional needs of each patient at the Resnick Neuropsychiatric Hospital.

FOR FURTHER RESEARCH

Books

Shari Brady, *It's Not What You're Eating, It's What's Eating You: A Teenager's Guide to Preventing Eating Disorders—and Loving Yourself*. New York: Skyhorse, 2018.

Maria Ganci and Linsey Atkins, *Letting Go of ED: Embracing Me; A Journal of Self-Discovery*. Melbourne, Australia: LM, 2019.

Maria Ganci and Linsey Atkins, *Unpack Your Eating Disorder: The Journey to Recovery for Adolescents in Treatment for Anorexia Nervosa and Atypical Anorexia Nervosa*. Melbourne, Australia: LM, 2019.

Cris E. Haltom et al., *Understanding Teen Eating Disorders*. New York: Routledge, 2018.

Amber Netting, *Intuitive Eating for Teens: The Teenager's Guide to Stop Dieting, Overcome Eating Disorders, Emotional and Binge Eating*. New York: Skyhorse, 2021.

Elyse Resch, *The Intuitive Eating Workbook for Teens: A Non-diet, Body Positive Approach to Building a Healthy Relationship with Food*. Oakland, CA: Instant Help, 2019.

Michele Siegel et al., *Surviving an Eating Disorder: Strategies for Family and Friends*. New York: HarperCollins, 2021.

Internet Sources

Cleveland Clinic, "Is Pandemic Stress Causing a Rise in Eating Disorders?," August 31, 2021. https://health.clevelandclinic.org.

Jane Feinmann, "Eating Disorders During the COVID-19 Pandemic," *British Medical Journal* 374, no. 1787 (2021). www.bmj.com.

Kathy Katella, "Eating Disorders on the Rise After Our Pandemic Year," Yale Medicine, June 15, 2021. www.yalemedicine.org.

Alana K. Otto et al., "Medical Admissions Among Adolescents with Eating Disorders During the COVID-19 Pandemic," *Pediatrics* 148, no. 4 (2021). https://publications.aap.org.

INDEX

PICTURE CREDITS

ABOUT THE AUTHOR

Katie Sharp has written many books for students. She lives in St. Louis, Missouri, with her two dogs, two cats, and a revolving door of foster animals.